Bail Yourself Out

*How You Can Emerge Strong
from the World Crisis*

LAITMAN
KABBALAH PUBLISHERS

Michael Laitman, PhD

BAIL YOURSELF OUT:
HOW YOU CAN EMERGE STRONG FROM THE WORLD CRISIS

Copyright © 2009 by MICHAEL LAITMAN
All rights reserved
Published by Laitman Kabbalah Publishers
www.kabbalah.info   info@kabbalah.info
1057 Steeles Avenue West, Suite 532, Toronto,
ON, M2R 3X1, Canada Bnei Baruch USA,
2009 85th Street #51, Brooklyn, New York, 11214, USA

Printed in Canada

Library of Congress Cataloging-in-Publication Data

Laitman, Michael.
Bail yourself out : How you can emerge strong from the world crisis /
Michael Laitman.
p. cm.
ISBN 978-1-897448-27-4
1. Self-help techniques. 2. Self-actualization (Psychology) 3.
Self-management (Psychology) 4. Human behavior. 5.
Economics–Psychological aspects. I. Title.
BF632.L32 2009

158–dc22   2009014508

Copy Editor: Claire Gerus
Associate Editors: Eli Vinokur, Riggan Shilstone
Proofreading: Michael R. Kellogg
Layout: Baruch Khovov
Cover Design: Richard Aquan,
Ole Færøvik, Therese Vadem
Printing and Post Production: Uri Laitman
Executive Editor: Chaim Ratz

FIRST EDITION: DECEMBER 2009
FIRST PRINTING

CONTENTS

The Seeds
of the Crisis

The global crisis we are all facing did not begin with the collapse of our financial system. It was actually in existence long before—rooted deep in human nature. To understand how we can bail ourselves out of this crisis, we need to understand why our own nature puts us on a collision course with nature and with each other.

1
WITH A MAP AND COMPASS, AND STILL LOST

It was about 9 a.m. when I parked my beat-up Toyota pickup at a parking lot on one of Mount Rainier's northern slopes, and my friend, Josh, and I stepped out of the truck. Our plan was to hike down to Cataract Valley, spend the night there, and hike out the next day. The forecast predicted a beautiful, sunny July day, and we were confident that by late afternoon we would be boiling water for supper at the camp.

Since we planned on being back at the parking lot the next day, our food and water supply was accordingly minimal. But once up in the mountains, you can never know. About an hour into the trail, the weather suddenly changed. Clouds came over the mountain and the view was hidden under a heavy fog. We knew that the trail would lead us down toward the valley, and hoped that the fog would clear as we descended, but we were wrong. Not only did the fog become so thick that we could barely see the trail beneath our feet, but the trail itself disappeared under sprawling snowfields, leaving us clueless as to where we were going.

Unable to see where we were heading and without a clear idea of our location, Josh and I were forced to rely on our limited navigation skills. Reluctantly, we turned to our map and compass for guidance (back then, a GPS was still a top-secret military device). We had two things going for us: we had a vague idea of where we were, and we knew our destination was (so aptly named) Cataract Valley. We hoped we could traverse the remaining five miles of rugged terrain with just our map and compass, but we were already becoming uneasy about our prospects.

We drew a straight line from our presumed position to the valley, set the compass arrow in that direction, and tried to follow it as best as we could.

We knew that at some point we would have to start descending toward the valley, but right now, we couldn't see more than twenty feet ahead, and the ground beneath us showed no sign of sloping. What made things worse was that the gentle meadow we'd been walking on had turned into boulder-strewn hills that forced us to watch our every step.

A few hours later, as dusk began to settle and our fears began to grow, the skies suddenly cleared for a moment. Right in front of us, where we had thought the descent toward the valley would be, appeared the snowy white summit of Mt. Rainier in all its glory.

This was when we realized that we were truly lost. Night was now approaching, and we did not have enough food and water to last us for many days. We knew the park rangers would not begin to search for us until our wilderness permit had expired by several days, and should one or both of us get hurt, we would not know where or how to get help.

As we nervously assessed our situation, our tense voices betrayed our anxiety and we soon began to blame each other for our predicament. For a few moments, our friendship was forgotten as our fears prevailed. But Josh and I had been friends for a long time, and we knew how to overcome trials. After a short, somber discussion, we vowed that we would find a trail the next morning come hell or high water, and we would find it together. Not wanting to stray any more than we had already, or run into a wandering bear, we decided to stay put and spend the night on the ridge.

To our relief, the next morning dawned with a sky as clear and as blue as the ocean on a summer day. Comparing the terrain in front of us to the terrain and trails marked on the map, we made an educated guess about our position. We realized that if we climbed down from the ridge, we would likely cross paths with one of the trails we saw on the map.

With hopeful hearts, we began the climb down. Three hours later, our knees barely supporting us from sliding down the steep and slippery mountainside (made even more treacherous by pine needles that cushioned the soil), we were elated to discover a human footprint in the mud. Then we found a trail. And very shortly after, we spotted a little wooden sign that read, "Cataract Valley."

Our sense of relief and joy was indescribable. We knew we were being given our lives back. But even more distinct was the awareness that it was our friendship and the fact that we stuck together that got us out of there. To me, Mount Rainier, and especially Cataract Valley, will forever be a testimony to the power of unity.

LESSONS FROM THE CRADLE OF CIVILIZATION

Today, as I reflect on the state of the world, my adventure on Mt. Rainier often comes to mind. In more ways than one, it can be seen as a strong parallel to our current situation.

When we look at the present state of humanity, it may seem quite grim, with a doubtful prognosis for success. But just as my friend and I were able to unite and emerge from the woods triumphant, we can be positive about the future of humanity. To guarantee our success, all we need is to unite and collaborate.

In fact, unity and collaboration have always been nature's, as well as humanity's tools for success. As this book will show, when we use them, we thrive, and when we avoid them, we break apart.

Thousands of years ago, between the rivers Euphrates and Tigris, in a vast and fertile stretch of land called "Mesopotamia," there lived a flourishing society in a city-state called "Babel." The city was bustling with life and action. It was the trade center of what we now call, "the cradle of civilization."

Befitting a civilization in its youth, Babel was a melting pot, filled with a variety of belief systems and teachings. Divination, card reading, face and palm reading, idol worship and many other esoteric practices were all common and accepted in Babel.

Among the most prominent and respected people in Babel was a man named Abraham. This man was a priest, an idol worshiper, and the son of an idol worshiper, but he was also a very perceptive and caring individual.

Abraham noticed that the people he loved so dearly were growing apart. Where there had been camaraderie among the townspeople of Babel, for no apparent reason, this feeling was gradually fading. Abraham felt that a hidden force had come into play, which was driving people away from one another. Yet, he could not understand where that force had come from and why it had not appeared before. In his search, Abraham began to question his beliefs and his way of life. He began to wonder how the world was built, how and why things were happening, and what was required of him so he could help his fellow citizens.

WISDOM IN THE TENT

Abraham, the inquisitive, thoughtful priest, was astonished to discover that the world runs on desires—two desires, to be exact: to give and to receive. He found that to create the world, these desires form a system of rules so profound and comprehensive that today we can only consider it a science. At the time, the term "science" did not exist, but Abraham had no need for a definition. Instead, he sought to explore these new rules and learn how they might help the people he loved.

Abraham found that these desires form a fabric that makes up our entire being. They determine not only our behavior, but the whole of reality—everything that we think, see, feel, taste, or touch. And the system of rules he had discovered created a mechanism that maintains the balance between them, so one would not exceed the other. These desires are dynamic and evolving, and Abraham realized that people were growing apart because the desire to receive within them had become stronger than the desire to give; it had become a desire for self-centered satisfaction, or egotism.

Abraham understood that the only way to reverse this trend was for people to unite, despite the growing egotism. He knew that a new level of bonding and camaraderie awaited his people beyond their rising suspicion of each other. However, to achieve this level, they had to unite. Now, Abraham knew that he had found the answer to his fellow Babylonians' unhappiness, and wished nothing more than for them to find it, too.

But to discover what he had discovered, and to regain their former sense of camaraderie and friendship, Abraham needed his people's cooperation. He knew he would not be able to help them unless they truly wanted his help. Although the people knew they were unhappy, they did not know why. Abraham's task, therefore, was to reveal to them why they were suffering.

Eager to begin, he set up a tent and invited everyone to come visit, eat and drink, and hear about the rules he had discovered.

Abraham was a famous man, a priest, and many came to hear him. But few were convinced, and the rest simply went on with their lives, seeking to sort out their problems in ways that were already familiar.

But Abraham's revolutionary discovery did not go unnoticed by the authorities, and soon he was confronted by no less than Nimrod, the ruler of Babel. In a famous debate between Abraham and Nimrod, who was well versed in the teachings of his time, Nimrod was bitterly defeated. Mortified, he sought revenge and tried to burn Abraham at the stake. However, Abraham escaped along with his family and fled from Babel.

Now leading a nomad's life, Abraham set up his tent wherever he went and invited local residents and passersby to hear about the rules he had discovered. In his journeys, he went through Haran, Canaan, Egypt, and finally back to Canaan.

To help convey what he had discovered, Abraham wrote the book we now know as *The Book of Creation*, where he introduced the essence of his revelations. Abraham's new purpose in life was to explain and expound on these discoveries to anyone who would listen. His sons, along with others who learned from him, created a dynasty of scholars that has been developing and implementing his method ever since. *The Book of Creation*, combined with the dedication of his students, ensured that Abraham's discoveries would live on from generation to generation, ultimately being available for implementation by the generation that truly needs them: our own!

3

THE CURRENTS OF DESIRE

When we reflect on humanity's state at the time of Babel, we can begin to understand why Nimrod rejected Abraham's revolutionary discovery. Even today, after humankind has spent centuries searching for the single, perfect formula that explains everything, Abraham's explanation of reality seems too simple to be true—until you begin to implement it.

As we said in the previous chapter, Abraham discovered that reality consists of two desires. One desire is to give and the other is to receive. He found that everything that has ever existed, that exists now, and that will exist is an outcome of the interaction between these two forces. When the desires work in harmony, life flows peacefully along its course. When they collide, however, we must deal with the fallout—calamities and crises of great magnitude.

Through these discoveries, Abraham understood how the universe and life had started, and how they evolve. Our universe was born approximately fourteen billion years ago, when a massive, never-again-repeated burst of energy exploded out of a minuscule point. Astronomers call it "the Big Bang." Just as a seed and an egg join to form an embryo at the moment of conception, the universe was "conceived" when the desire to give and the desire to receive were first joined together in the Big Bang. For this reason, all that exists in our universe is a manifestation of the joining of the two forces.

Just as a cell in an embryo begins to divide and create the flesh of the newborn immediately after conception, the desire to give and the desire to receive began to form the matter of our universe immediately after the Big Bang. Then, through a process that spanned billions of years, and that to an extent continues today, gases alternately expanded and contracted, galaxies were created, and stars were formed within them. Every expansion of gas was a consequence of the desire to give, which expands and creates, and every contraction was the result of the desire to receive, which absorbs and contracts.

Humanity, like the universe, is a perfect system comprised of myriad elements that interact with each other. Just as billions of galaxies make up the universe, billions of people combine to make up humanity. And just as there are stars within each galaxy, there are people within nations and states. And the organs, tissue, and cells within each person's body are like the planets, comets, and asteroids orbiting their suns.

Expansion and contraction form the endless ebb and flow of life, propelled at one moment by the desire to give, and at the next moment by the desire to receive. Whether it is galaxies, suns, and planets merging to form our universe, or cells, tissue, and organs combining to form a human being, this interplay of desires is at the heart of creation.

As with the stars, Planet Earth evolved by expansion and contraction through the interaction of desires. When Earth was first formed, its surface reflected the flow of expansion and the ebb of contraction. Every time the desire to give prevailed, Earth's sweltering interior would burst into rivers of melted lava. And every time the receiving force prevailed, the lava would cool and form new swaths of land. Eventually, a strong enough crust was formed over the Earth to allow for the emergence of life as we know it.

If we search deep enough, we will find the same two forces—giving and receiving—within every being ever created, weaving their magnificent garment of life. In the weaving process, the desire to give first creates matter, as with the Big Bang or a newborn baby, and the desire to receive gives the matter shape, as with the stars and the differentiating cells in organisms.

THE BIRTH OF LIFE

The story does not end with the creation of the universe. When a baby is born, it cannot control its hands or legs, which seem to move about erratically. However, there is tremendous importance in these seemingly erratic movements: after many repetitions, the baby gradually learns which movements get results and which do not. Unless the baby tries, it will not learn how to turn over, crawl, and eventually walk. In a baby, the life force (the desire to give) creates movement. But it is the desire to receive that gives that force direction and determines which expressions of the desire to give (movements) should stay and which should not.

The same principle can be applied to Earth's early childhood. As the earth was cooling, particles driven by the desire to give moved randomly about. The desire to receive caused these particles to contract and form clusters, and only the most stable of these groups survived, forming atoms.

Atoms, too, moved about randomly because the desire to give within them was tossing them erratically, and the desire to receive gradually formed more sustainable groups of atoms. Those were the first molecules. From here, the road to the first living creature was paved.

In children, the desires to give and to receive appear in ways best suited to their needs. First, babies develop motor capabilities, enabling them to suckle from their mother's breast or grasp their father's little finger. Then, social skills such as a smile or a frown emerge. Eventually, they develop language and more complex capabilities. In each case, the desire to give generates the movement and energy, and the desire to receive determines its ultimate form.

During creation, these desires cooperated to create increasingly complex creatures. Uni-cellular creatures came first. Then, these creatures learned to cooperate so they would increase their chances of survival. Some cells excelled in breathing and became in charge of providing oxygen to all the other cells. Other cells learned to digest effectively and became responsible for providing nutrients to the rest of the cells in the "colony." Some cells learned to think for everyone else and became the "colony's" brain.

Thus, multi-cellular creatures were formed where each cell had a unique role and responsibility, and depended on the rest of the cells for its livelihood. This quality is what characterizes complex creatures such as plants, animals, and most notably, man.

THE DAWN OF HUMANITY

Layer by layer, life evolved peacefully in its course. Then came humans. The first humans were more like apes. They ate what they found on the ground or in the trees, and they hunted what they could. They cooperated, but they acted purely on instinct.

But humans are not like other animals. They discovered that to increase their chances of survival, they should focus on developing their intellect rather than their bodies. As a result, they learned how to make weapons for hunting, instead of using their hands or rocks. They also learned how to use vessels for gathering and storing food. Over time, humans improved the use of their intellect, which enhanced their chances of survival even more. Thus, gradually, the human race became ruler of the earth.

The ability to use tools to increase food production and to build better shelters offered us a unique possibility, unavailable to other creatures: we found we could change our environment to fit our needs, instead of changing ourselves to fit nature's dictates. This has been the key element in the evolution of humanity ever since.

The realization that we could change our surroundings to suit our desires changed the future of the human race forever. We were no longer dependent on nature, but on our own resourcefulness. That tipping point was the birth of what we now refer to as "civilization."

The dawn of civilization, approximately ten thousand years ago, was beautiful. We improved our hunting tools, developed agriculture, invented the wheel, and saw life merrily rolling along from good to better. The only hitch in the ability to constantly improve our lives was that this ability made us feel far more powerful than we really are; we began to feel superior to nature, and this would prove to be the root of all ills.

4

THE SECRET OF THE TWO DESIRES

In the previous chapter, we said that the desire to give creates matter, and the desire to receive gives it shape. Humans are no exception to the rule: we receive our life energy from the desire to give, and we are formed by the desire to receive. However, since we learned that we could change our surroundings to suit our desires, we have been focusing entirely on the desire to receive. We have become ignorant of the fact that we receive energy and life not from the desire to receive, but from the desire to give.

Human beings are a special species: since we realized that we could change our surroundings to our benefit, we have been developing increasingly sophisticated ways to do so. We have learned that we can use our intelligence, instead of our physical strength, to enhance our pleasure.

Yet, to enhance it effectively, we need to know what parts of nature we can change, when we can change them, and how. For example, agriculture is a change of nature because instead of picking wild oats, for instance, we can domesticate them, grow them in a field, produce many more of them, and collect them more easily. But to avoid doing harm to the environment, farmers must take into consideration numerous pieces of information, to make certain that they do not jeopardize its overall balance.

And to be able to maintain that balance, we must be aware of all the elements involved in the making of the environment, and first and foremost, of the desire to give and the desire to receive, and how they interact. Otherwise, it is as if we were trying to build a house without knowing how to make a strong and stable foundation, or planning the number of rooms without knowing how many people will be living in it.

The interplay between the two desires eludes us because it is the very basis of our make up, and therefore resides at a level deeper even than our consciousness. But once we understand how these desires interact with each other to create life, we can put this information into practice and discover how to benefit from doing so.

At the same time, if we build our lives taking both desires into account, our common sense will often be challenged. We will find ourselves considering actions and attitudes that seem to make no sense to our desire to receive, which wants *only* to receive. For example, what good would it do for me to give something to someone that I don't know, don't care for, and who would never return my favor? It makes no sense to my desire to receive.

If you suggested that by doing so I would come to know the other half of reality—the desire to give—and that I would understand how the force that creates life works, I would probably suggest that you needed to see a therapist, rather than recognize that what you are telling me has value.

When you think about it, it is very easy to sympathize with Nimrod, the ruler of ancient Babel. In all likelihood, he wished for nothing more than to protect his subjects from Abraham, the anarchist. Abraham preached unity as a cure for the growing alienation and separation plaguing the residents of Babel. He proposed that the only reason that the kinship between people was dissipating was that they were unaware of the existence of the other desire that creates life—the desire to give. If they knew it, he tried to tell them, they could relate to one another in a more balanced way, and reap the harvest of experiencing the whole of reality, with both its desires.

But because no one else was fortunate enough to make this discovery in Babel besides Abraham, he appeared more like an eccentric than a redeemer. Nimrod thought that Abraham's arguments were not only senseless, but threatened the order of life in his domain. And the fact that he was the son of a renowned and respected idol maker made Nimrod even more concerned. People were merrily worshiping their idols, and Nimrod did not want to interrupt their way of life. He couldn't see that their days as a happy community were numbered.

Hence, Nimrod took to the path of denial, and the vast majority of his subjects followed him— to their eventual ruin.

LIKE A MOTHERLESS CHILD

To understand why our ignorance of the desire to give is so harmful, we can think of the relationship between the desire to give and the desire to receive like the relationship between a mother and her child. In a healthy relationship, the baby knows her mother and knows to whom to turn when she is hungry, cold, or tired. But what if the baby had no mother? To whom would she turn to satisfy her needs? Who would feed her, clothe her, keep her warm and love her? She would have to take care of herself. What would the chances of survival be for such a poor child?

Ever since that fateful day when Nimrod chased Abraham out of Babel, some 4,000 years ago, humanity has been like that baby, trying to lead life as best as it could. We have muddled along, but we have detached ourselves from the desire to give, the life-giving force that nurtures us and the rest of the universe.

Like a motherless child, we have been deprived of guidance, trying to learn how to survive by trial and error. In our efforts to find a sustainable order in life, we have tried living in clans, slavery, Greek democracy, feudalism, capitalism, communism, modern democracy, fascism, and even Nazism. We have sought solace for our fears of the unknown in religion, mysticism, philosophy, science, technology, art, and, in fact, in every area of human engagement. All of these ideologies and pursuits promised us a happy life; none have kept that promise.

Without being aware of the desire to give and the need to balance ourselves with it, as do all other elements in nature, we have been acting solely on our desire to receive. Thus, we have created deformed societies rampant with exploitation and tyranny.

It is true that humanity has made many great achievements, such as modern medicine and abundant food and energy production. But the more we have advanced, the more we have misused our achievements, ever widening the gaps between us and increasing social injustice.

It is no one's fault that human societies are deformed and inherently unjust. Without knowing about the desire to give, we are left with but one option in life: to receive what we can whenever possible. Hence, those who are exploited today will be exploiting tomorrow, if they come into power, because when we work with only the desire to receive, then all we want is to receive.

5

INSATIABLE HUMANITY

Our imperiled world is indeed a sad result of man's lack of recognition of the desire to give. In contrast, the rest of nature is a magnificent display of balance between the two desires. In the diverse ecosystem that is Planet Earth, each creature has its unique role. The system is incomplete if even a single element in it is missing or deficient, be it a mineral, a plant, or an animal.

An eye-opening report submitted to the U.S. Department of Education in October, 2003 by Irene Sanders and Judith McCabe, PhD, clearly demonstrates what happens when we breach nature's balance. "In 1991, an orca—a killer whale—was seen eating a sea otter. Orcas and otters usually coexist peacefully. So, what happened? Ecologists found that ocean perch and herring were also declining. Orcas don't eat those fish, but seals and sea lions do. And seals and sea lions are what orcas usually eat, and their population had also declined. So deprived of their seals and sea lions, orcas started turning to the playful sea otters for dinner.

So otters have vanished because the fish, which they never ate in the first place, have vanished. Now, the ripple spreads, otters are no longer there to eat sea urchins, so the sea urchin population has exploded. But sea urchins live off seafloor kelp forests, so they're killing off the kelp. Kelp has been home to fish that feed seagulls and eagles. Like orcas, seagulls can find other food, but bald eagles can't and they're in trouble.

All this began with the decline of ocean perch and herring. Why? Well, Japanese whalers have been killing off the variety of whales that eat the same microscopic organisms that feed pollock [a type of carnivorous fish]. With more fish to eat, pollock flourish. They in turn attack the perch and herring that were food for the seals and sea lions. With the decline in the population of sea lions and seals, the orcas must turn to otters."

Thus, true health and well being are achieved only when there is harmony and balance among *all* the parts that make up an organism or a system. Yet, we are so unaware of the other force in life, the giving force, that we cannot achieve this balance, or even positively define what being "healthy" means.

The definition of health in the Britannica Concise Encyclopedia truly captures our sense of bafflement: "Good health is harder to define than bad health (which can be equated with presence of disease) because it must convey a more positive concept than mere absence of disease." But because we have no perception of the positive force in life, we cannot define a positive state of existence.

We all have dreams, and we all wish for them to come true. But the sad truth is that we never feel that we have realized all our dreams because even if we fulfill them, new ones step in to replace those we have fulfilled. As a result, *we never feel satisfied*. And the more we strive for wealth, power, fame, and everything else we deem pleasurable, the more dissatisfied we become, and the more disillusioned.

Thus, the more we have, the more frustrated and disillusioned we are because we will have tried harder to find happiness and will have failed more often, and possibly more bitterly. This explains why richer countries generally suffer from higher depression rates.

Ironically, there is a positive aspect to depression. It is an indication that we have given up on Nimrod's way of focusing solely on our desire to receive. People who are depressed are those who see no prospect of joy or happiness in the future. They are too experienced in life's failures to be lured into yet another failed attempt at happiness. But all they need to cure their depression is to realize that there is another half of reality, the "giving half." If we can help these people see that they have been trying to suck joy out of a vacuum—a desire to receive—a force that knows only how to receive and not how to give, it will bring back all the hope and energy that they lost to depression.

Indeed, reality is a two-legged creature, and we have been using only one of them. Why, then, are we surprised that it reality is lame?

6
Cellular Unity

Like Josh and me on Mount Rainier, humanity has been lost in the wilderness for generations. Like Josh and me, humanity did not heed the first warning signs of impending trouble. And like Josh and me, humanity kept on going, relying on what tools it had, although it has been blind to half of reality, as if a mist (or cataract) had covered its eyes. This is why today we are in such a massive, global crisis.

But the part that reminds me most of my personal ordeal is the fact that the only way out of this crisis is *with each other*. This time, it truly is survival for all, or for no one at all.

The average adult human body contains roughly ten trillion cells (10,000,000,000,000). Placed side by side, they would circle the earth 47 times! Not one of them is autonomous. Instead, they all work in perfect harmony to support and sustain the body they live in, sometimes at the expense of their own lives. As a result, their "awareness" stretches far beyond their cell membranes and encompasses the whole body. The harmony between cells is what makes a healthy body such a perfect and beautiful machine.

A healthy body has such an effective maintenance mechanism that if even a single cell were to neglect its duties and work for itself, the body would detect that cell and then heal it or kill it. Without yielding to the dominion of the body, no organism could ever be created because its cells would not be able to cooperate and work for the good of the whole body.

In fact, a cell that works for itself instead of for the body is called a "cancerous cell." When such cells succeed in multiplying, a person develops cancer. The end result of cancer is always the death of the tumor. The only unknown is whether the tumor will die because it was killed by the body or by the drugs, or because it killed its host body, thus killing itself. Whether we are aware of it or not, when we act for ourselves, disregarding the needs of the whole, we become cancerous cells in the body called "humanity."

Before we realized we could change the environment to fit our needs, we were healthy cells in humanity, in natural harmony with the call of nature. But once we realized we could "bend" nature to our benefit, we divorced ourselves from that harmony. Therefore, to avoid disrupting nature's balance, we have to become consciously harmonious with it.

However, we haven't yet been able to do so. Because we've been unaware of the interplay between the desire to give and desire to receive, we have been taking nature for granted, believing that it would be there for us regardless of our behavior.

In complex, integrated systems, the rule is that the system dictates and the individual yields, just as with the example of cells in a body. As humanity grew in numbers and began to build increasingly complex societies, our need to match the rules of integrated systems became more pressing.

NIMROD'S WAY

Naturally, Nimrod did not want to accept the rule of integrated systems that Abraham introduced. He was the ruler of Babel, and yet here was one of his subjects telling him that he, the ruler of the greatest land in the world, must yield to a higher law than his own.

True to human nature's egotism, Nimrod could not concede that his way, and that of his fathers, of following the desire to receive, had been wrong, and that changes were required. To preserve the way humanity has been building itself up to that point, Nimrod had no other choice but to try to eliminate the risk. He took the course of action that the human race has used since the day weapons were first invented, and decided to destroy Abraham.

Although he did not manage to kill Abraham, he did chase him out of Babel. But Nimrod's Babel was too big a city to exist without applying the rule of integrated systems. And without knowing how to unite the people of Babel, all of whom were acting on their desires to receive, the Babylonians could not stay together and the beautiful megalopolis disintegrated.

7

STEPPING OFF THE MOUNT

Had Josh and I parted on Mount Rainier, I might not have been writing these words today. Lucky for me, our friendship endured. (Also helpful was the fact that we only had one compass and one map, so it wasn't as if we had other options). But from the moment we decided to pull out of our plight together, we sensed such a great relief that it was as if we had already found the trail.

Admittedly, the descent from the ridge was not easy. It took my knees months to recover from the effort, and my back was never quite the same

again. But I will always treasure our sense of togetherness as we carefully slid down the treacherous mountainside, checking constantly to be sure
that the other was all right.

A few minutes into the descent, we found ourselves surrounded by a thick forest that swallowed
up the sunlight. Behind us was the mountain, and
far ahead and far below us was the bottom of the
ravine. And we, together, were climbing down a
slope more precipitous than I could ever imagine.
Occasionally, I would stop to rest my knees on a
rock that bulged above the needles, and I would
gaze in awe at the trees, thinking, "They must be
fastened to the ground with nails. There is no other way to explain how they remain standing."

As we were literally hanging by our nails to
the ground to keep from falling, the power of our
bond supported us. Today, I know that this is what
got us through.

An old song that I used to like as a child says
that only in the mountains do you know who your
true friends are. Now I know exactly what that
song meant.

But the crisis we're all facing today requires
a unity that goes beyond friendship between individuals. Uniting all parts of humanity has far
deeper implications than saving the lives of a few
adventurers. We need to unite not because it is

more fun (although it is), but because we need to discover the desire to give, the part of nature we have been oblivious to for millennia, and the only way to discover it is to emulate it. When we emulate it, we will suddenly discover that it actually exists in every aspect of our lives, from our cells to our minds.

As sentient beings, we can only perceive the existence of something when we feel it. We live in an "ocean" composed of the desire to give, but we can only feel this desire when it is "dressed" in some palpable form of pleasure. We naturally focus on the pleasure we derive from objects or incidents that cross our path through life, but it is never only the desire to receive there. Instead, it is a combination of the two: the desire to give creates a new sense of possible pleasure, and the desire to receive shapes that pleasure in the form of, say, a delicious piece of cake, a new friend, making love, or making money.

But the new emergence of the desire to give that we are sensing today is no ordinary emergence. This desire is not for sex, money, power, or fame. This time, it is a *desire for connectedness*. This is the underlying motive behind the massive growth of social networks on the Internet. People need to connect because they already feel connected; now, they just need to know how to do so in a way that truly fills their needs. However, the only way to feel completely connected is to study the force that binds all individuals into one: the desire to give.

So without further ado, let us see how we can bring the desire to give into our lives.

II

Learning
from
Nature

The surest way to correct mistakes is to learn from those who have done things right. In this case, nature is our role model and a proven success, so she should be our teacher.

8

A Way Out of the Woods

To see how we can let the desire to give into our lives, let's look at how nature does it. We perceive the outside world by using our senses, and we believe that the picture of reality our senses provide is accurate and reliable. But is it?

How often do we walk with a friend, and the friend hears something that we miss? Well, just because we didn't hear that sound doesn't mean there was none. All it means is that our senses didn't pick it up, or that we didn't pay attention. Or maybe our friend was hallucinating!

In all three possibilities, the objective reality is the same, but our perception of it is not. In other words, we do not know what the actual reality is like, or if it even exists. All we know is what we *perceive* of it.

So how do we perceive? We use a process best described as "equivalence of form." Each of our senses responds to a different type of stimulus, but all our senses work in a similar manner. When a ray of light, for instance, penetrates my pupil, the neurons in my retina create a model of the outside image. This model is then encoded and transferred to my brain, which decodes the pulses and reconstructs the image. A similar process occurs when a sound hits our eardrums or when something touches our skin.

In other words, my brain uses my senses to create a model or form equal to the outside object. But if my model is inaccurate, I will never know it and will believe that the actual object or sound is the same as the model I created in my mind.

The "equivalence of form" principle applies not only to our senses, but to our behavior, as well. Children, for example, learn by repeating behavior they see in their surroundings. We call this "imitation." Eager to learn about the world they were born into, and having no language skills, children use imitation as a means to acquire skills such as sitting and standing, speech, and use of cutlery. When we speak, they watch how we move our lips. This is why parents are advised to speak clearly to children (but not loudly; they can hear better than we). By imitating us, children create the same forms (movements or sounds) as we do, and thus learn about the world they live in.

In fact, not only do children learn that way, but the whole of nature is a testimony to the efficiency of learning through equivalence of form. It is thrilling to watch lion cubs play. They crouch in ambush, attacking each other with the enthusiasm of youth. They stalk everything from shadows to insects to antelopes. There is little danger of their actually catching anything at this stage, but for them, stalking is not mere play. By assuming the role of hunter, they act out a function they will have to execute very seriously as adults. Acting is how they bring the hunter within them to life. Without it, they will not survive because they will not know how to bring down the prey that will feed and sustain them.

If we wish to perceive the desire to give, all we need do is to create an image of it within us. If we pay close attention to our thoughts and desires while performing acts of giving, we will discover within us a desire that is equal to the desire to give that exists in nature. Then, as naturally as children discover speech by emulating sounds and syllables, we will discover the desire to give by emulating giving.

It may take a while before we know how to balance receiving and giving as nature does it, but practice makes perfect and we will succeed. And when we have done so, our lives will be a boundless flow of revelations so profound and rich we will be in awe at how blind we could have been thus far.

In today's world, we can no longer be oblivious to the workings of the desire to give. We are not in Babel, where people could avoid friction between them by moving away and spreading to the outlands. Because we have populated every corner of the globe, we have nowhere to go. In addition, we have connected ourselves so tightly to each other that it would be easier to unscramble scrambled eggs than to undo our global connections.

And this is not a bad thing. Without global connections, where would we get such inexpensive goods as those provided by China and India? And who would give work and bread to the workers in those countries? Now that the world economy is going through a mammoth downturn, we can see how beneficial globalization can be if we use it properly.

Actually, the world is the same megalopolis that it was in the times of Babel, but now we are that megalopolis on a global scale. We cannot disperse, so we must either unite or destroy each other. We are a single whole, one body, and we must learn to act the part. The more we put off doing so, the less healthy we and our society will become.

So, to avoid destroying each other, let us all resolve that we are going to come out of this crisis *together*. On Mount Rainier, Josh and I did not like each other at that moment of distress, but we decided to *act as if we did*. And to our surprise, it worked.

On the mountain, there were just the two of us. We could just sit down and talk to each other. To succeed on a global scale, we need a global means of communication to communicate the concept of togetherness. To this end, we will now take a look at the media.

9

CREATING A MEDIA THAT CARES

The media must play a key role in shifting the public atmosphere from alienation to camaraderie. The media provides us with almost everything we know about our world. Even the information we receive from friends or from family usually arrives via the media. It is the modern version of the grapevine.

But media does not simply provide us with information. It also offers us tidbits about people we approve or disapprove of, and we form our views based on what we see, hear, or read on the media. Because its power over the public is unrivaled, if the media turns to togetherness and unity, the world will follow.

Regrettably, until the outbreak of the financial crisis, the media has been focusing on successful individuals, media moguls, mega pop stars, and ultra-successful individuals who made millions and billions at the expense of their competitors. Only recently, as an offshoot of the crisis, has the media begun to display acts of compassion and unity, such as the sandbagging efforts by thousands of volunteers in Fargo, North Dakota, who joined forces in March, 2009 to stop the highest cresting of the Red River in recorded history.

While this trend is certainly welcome, a few sporadic and spontaneous efforts are not enough to truly bring people together. To really change our worldview, to make us aware of the existence of the desire to give, the media should present the full picture of reality, and inform us of its structure. To this end, it should create programs that demonstrate how the desire to give affects all levels of nature—inanimate, vegetative, animate, and human—and encourage people to emulate it. Instead of talk shows that host people who only talk about themselves, why not host people who praise others? After all, such examples abound; we just have to acknowledge them and bring them to the public's attention.

If the media shows people caring for each other, and explains that such images will help us let the giving force into our lives, it will shift the public's focus from self-centeredness to camaraderie. Today, the most popular viewpoint should be, "Unity is fun—let's join the party."

At the risk of making some gross generalizations, here are a few facts and numbers to think about: Our computers and TVs are made in China and Taiwan; our cars are made in Japan, Europe, and the U.S., and our clothes are made in India and China. Also, almost everyone watches Hollywood films, and by the end of this year (2009), China will have more English speakers than any other country in the world.

And here is a really interesting concept: Facebook, the online social network, has 200 million active users worldwide. If Facebook were a country, it would be the fifth largest country in the world!

Indeed, globalization is a fact, and it is showing us that we are already united. We can try to resist it, or we can join in and benefit from the diversity, opportunities, and abundance that globalization has in store for us.

There are ample ways the media can show us that unity is a gift. Although every scientist knows that no system in nature operates in isolation and that interdependency is the name of the game, most of us are unaware of it. When we see how every organ works to benefit the whole body, how bees collaborate in hives, how a school of fish swims in such unison that it can even be mistaken for a giant fish, how wolves hunt together, and how chimpanzees help other chimps, or even humans, without any reward in return, we will know that nature's primary law is harmony and coexistence.

The media can and should show us such examples far more often than it does. When we realize that this is how nature works, we will spontaneously examine our societies and see if they are in unison with this harmony.

If our thoughts begin to shift in this direction, they will create a different atmosphere and introduce a spirit of hope and strength into our lives, even before we actually implement that spirit. Why? Because we will be aligned with nature's life force—the desire to give.

The more connected we feel to others, the more our happiness depends on how they feel about us. If others approve of our actions and views, we feel good about ourselves. If they disapprove of what we do or say, we will feel bad about ourselves, hide our actions or even modify them to suit the social norm. In other words, because it is so important for us to feel good about ourselves, the media is in a unique position to shift people's actions and views.

Not surprisingly, politicians are the most ratings-dependent people on earth, as their very livelihood depends on their popularity. If we show them that we have changed our values, they will change theirs to follow our lead. And one of the easiest, most effective ways to tell them what we value is to show them what we want to watch on TV! Because politicians want to stay in office, we need to show them that if they want to retain their positions, they must promote what we want them to promote—unity.

When we are able to create media that promotes unity and collaboration instead of self-glorification of celebrities, we will create an environment that persuades us that unity and balance between the desires are good.

WATERS OF LOVE

A wise man once said that our hearts are like stones, and our good deeds towards each other are like waters that fall right at the center of those stones. Bit by bit, the waters carve a crater in one's heart, into which an abundance of love can pour.

As we have said throughout this book, the desire to give is the source of all pleasure in life, and the desire to receive is what shapes that pleasure. Through the good we do for others, we create in them a desire to receive more pleasure from being loved.

Of course, we all want to be loved, but very few of us believe that it will ever happen. But if we decide collectively to give love to each other, even if we don't actually feel it, we will rekindle in our fellow men and women the conviction that love is possible. And they will give it back, but for real, because this is what they will feel in their newly softened hearts.

All this may sound unscientific and irrational, but it works because it is in harmony with life's most fundamental forces—the desire to give and the desire to receive. And since we can always use some extra help when exploring unfamiliar territory, there are several techniques that can increase our chances of success. The rest of the chapters in this book will provide a view of what life would be like in a balanced world.

Achieving
Equilibrium

The following chapters will outline our escape route from the current crisis. They will touch on six basic aspects of life—arts, economy, education, politics, health, and climate—and will offer guidelines as to how we can use the desire to give to our benefit.

10

HOW THE ARTS CAN MODEL NEW ATTITUDES

"We all know that art is not truth. Art is a lie that makes us realize truth, at least the truth that is given us to understand. The artist must know the manner whereby to convince others of the truthfulness of his lies."

--Pablo Picasso

As important as media is to our culture, it cannot make the required shift in spirit all by itself. To complete the shift in our thinking, we must engage actors, singers, and other public idols and celebrities in the process. Their productions are displayed not only on television, but also on the Internet, in movie theatres, and on the radio, and are vital to getting the new message across.

It is hard to predict exactly how the arts will develop once we become familiar with the giving half of reality. Because we have never tried it on a large scale, we cannot tell how things will unfold once unity and giving are in vogue. The ideas below will describe possible shifts in cinema and theatre, but the rules that apply to this art form also apply to the more traditional arts such as painting and sculpturing.

The visual arts are the most powerful means of influence. Up to 90 percent of the information we receive on our surroundings is visual information. For this reason, a shift in our thinking must begin with what we see, even before we change what we hear.

On the surface, the plots of most movies and plays can remain pretty much the same: a fight for a just cause, a love story, or even a tragedy. But behind each plot should be a subtext that conveys a message of unity.

Today, when we leave the theatre or shut off the DVD, we are usually left with a sense of admiration for the hero. It is very rare that we contemplate an idea, a concept or an ideology after the movie. This often happens even if the movie does convey an idea, because the props, visual effects, script, and other elements in the film aim to create identification with a person, not with a way of life.

If we examine the plots of most blockbusters, we will arrive at an inevitable conclusion: heroes sell, ideas don't. This may have been true until recently, but in today's reality, people will need movies and plays either to forget about their troubles or to muster strength and hope for the future. And if done right, the latter will prevail by far.

If we watch movies from the 1950s and 60s, they often seem naïve to us, a bit out of touch with the "real life." Quite soon, viewers will watch the films made today and see them as out of touch, too. To succeed, art must reflect current situations, and today's news is unity, or balance, between the desire to receive and the desire to give.

There have been many apocalyptic films describing how humanity has destroyed the planet and is being punished for its sins with chaos, endless heat waves, war, and depletion of food and water. But art should not confine itself to doomsday images. Instead, it should provide information about the full picture of reality—the two forces in life, how they interact, what happens if we tip the balance, and what happens if we help to sustain it. Otherwise, arts, and especially the very popular visual arts, will not achieve their objectives: to inform us of life's two forces and to show us how we can balance them.

FILMS OF HOPE

To give people a reason to watch and re-watch movies and plays, the plots must be credible, providing *valid* hope and a real prospect of positive change. While a film's starting point can be our current reality, it must include some form of reasoning about what brought us to our current state. When people discover that the cinema has become a place where they can get information that will improve their lives, they will begin to flock to the movies!

Think of how we teach our children to cross the street, how meticulously and lovingly we explain to them time and time again how to wait for the green light, and how to only cross at designated crossings. This is vital information, and without it, they could risk their lives if they were to venture alone on the street.

Today, information about restoring balance in nature and in humanity is just as vital, and hence in high demand.

But there is more to this shift than survival. This crisis is a springboard for unfathomable improvement in our daily lives. Until today, we have been focusing on how much we can receive. In fact, we did not even know that we were being run by a desire to receive; we simply wanted to enjoy. Because we did not know about the interplay between the two desires that make up life, we kept searching for pleasure at a superficial level, and hence never experienced lasting joy and happiness.

But life's drama evolves in two directions (which are both opposite and parallel): collaboration and self-fulfillment. In the whole of reality, self-fulfillment is possible *only* through collaboration with others.

In minerals, for example, different atoms collaborate to form the molecules of that mineral. If one of the atoms were to separate, the mineral would disintegrate.

At a higher level of complexity, in plants and animals (including humans), there is a collaboration of different molecules, cells, and organs. These unite to create a distinct creature, and here, too, if even one of the molecules were missing in that creature's cells, it would become sick or even die.

In much the same way, all the plants and animals in a certain geographical area create a symbiotic environment. As with the story of the orcas and the otters we described in Chapter 5, *all* creatures contribute to maintaining the balance of that ecosystem. If even one of them were to dwindle in numbers, the system would be thrown off balance. Put simply, nature supports and promotes uniqueness; therefore, the personal fulfillment of creatures is possible only when they collaborate and contribute to their environment. When they want to develop themselves at the expense of the environment, nature will either extinguish them or forcefully balance their numbers.

Although we have known this law of nature for a long time, we have been acting as if we were not part of the ecosystem called "Planet Earth." Even worse, among ourselves we feel that one society or sect can be superior to another. Yet nature evidently demonstrates that *nothing* is redundant and no part of any element in nature is superior to another. Why, then, do we think we have a prerogative that no other part of nature has—to patronize and oppress other peoples and species? Where has this arrogance come from, if not from ignorance?

Because we are ignorant of the desire to give, which gives us our strength and wisdom, we relate them to ourselves. If we were aware that we, too, are a product of the two desires that form life, we would know how to thrive in this world, along with the whole of nature.

How difficult is it to make films that teach us this, and show us the benefits of self-fulfillment through collaboration? Imagine that we all knew that we were united with all other people, that we were supported by all other people in the world, and that all they wanted was for us to realize our potential to the maximum? How wonderful would life be if every person contributed all of his or her talents to society, and received the support and appreciation of society in return?

After all, is it not what we are already doing? A computer engineer contributes to society by building computers. A street sweeper contributes by cleaning streets. Which of them is more important? If we remembered that we did not become who we are by some act of will on our part, but because of a grand system and a primordial power working within us, we would not feel compelled to constantly prove ourselves. Instead, we would simply enjoy being who we are, and contribute what and where we can. We would actually enjoy being part of humanity—united and unique at the same time.

Imagine the movies showing us that!

11

Finding Balance in Song and Melody

"The new sound-sphere is global. It ripples at great speed across languages, ideologies, frontiers and races. The economics of this musical Esperanto is staggering. ...Popular music has brought with it sociologies of private and public manner, of group solidarity."

--George Steiner

Music is one of the most popular art forms; it can be a powerful promoter of new concepts. Today, more than ever, genres such as rock and hip-hop are powerful means of expressing social concepts. Ever since The Beatles introduced Indian music in the 1960s, ethnic music has been a popular means of promoting ethnic recognition and cultural integration. Indeed, globalization is a welcome addition to music, and today most musicians play several types of music, some of which come from cultures outside their homelands. Thus, music merits a chapter all to itself.

Like all forms of art, music is a special language that expresses the particular artist's inner world. Each type of music represents a different type of desire to receive, and can therefore express a different type of balance with the desire to give. To keep it simple, let's divide music into two groups: vocal and instrumental.

SONGS OF ENDLESS LOVE

With vocal music (songs), it is slightly easier to define the change required for it to fit into the new direction. As with cinema, the themes can remain pretty much the same. And as with cinema, behind each song should be a subtext that conveys a message of unity and expresses *both* desires in reality—to give and to receive.

Music is an expression of the self, of the deepest emotions of the artist. Therefore, if music is to convey a message of unity and balance between giving and receiving, it is very important that the performing artist be well aware of how these forces interact. Because we cannot fake how we express our inner world, artists must personally experience the unity and the interplay and connectedness of the two forces, if they are to convey them artistically.

As a result, every song should convey a new sense of freshness and vitality. There is no need to create new genres. We already have a wonderful variety: pop, hip-hop, rock n' roll, jazz, classical music, and ethnic music of every type. All are genuine expressions of our inner being, and there is no need to change them. All we need to change is the underlying message: instead of focusing on a couple's troubled relationship, the words can highlight their efforts to discover the unity in *nature*.

As we learn about the giving side of nature, we will also be able to create new texts for songs. Such texts can express dialogues between the desire to give and the desire to receive as they occur between people or in nature. If you think about it, the constant drive of the desire to give to find ways to express itself through the desire to receive is very similar to the way a man seeks new ways to express his love for his woman (or the other way around). What could be more inspiring than to dress that ache of love in lyrics and adorn it with a melody?

MELODIES OF HARMONY

Instrumental music is a different tune altogether. The focus on harmony in Western music makes it an almost natural medium to convey unity and balance. Many famed composers—most notably Bach and Mozart—paid close attention to keeping their music balanced and harmonious. In fact, classical music is so well balanced and wholesome that the University of Leicester, UK, found that it increases milk production in dairies! Although the composers were probably unaware of the depth to which this balance goes, or the purposes for which their music would one day be used, it is this quality that has assured their popularity up to the present day.

But balance exists not only in Western music; it is essential to almost any type of music, especially indigenous music. Today, however, balance must be kept not just because we like the sound of it, but because it can help us express a whole new side of reality. The result can be extremely passionate, extremely soft, extremely fast, or well tempered. But whatever the genre, the impact of such music on the listener will be unmatched, precisely because it expresses our life force!

Today, the music of Bach, Mozart, Beethoven, and Verdi seems rich and colorful to us. But compared to music that expresses the perception of *both* desires, it will be like the difference between seeing the world in only two dimensions, or in three.

12

MONEY, MONEY, MONEY

"Despite massive wealth creation, happiness has not risen since the 1950s in the US or Britain... No researcher questions these facts. So accelerated economic growth is not a goal for which we should make large sacrifices. In particular, we should not sacrifice the most important source of happiness, which is the quality of human relationships—at home, at work, and in the community."

--Richard Layard,
The Financial Times,
March 11, 2009

No aspect of our lives better expresses our interconnectedness than the economy. When we are united, the economy is the first to thrive and boosts every aspect of our lives along with it. But when we are separated from each other, it is the first to collapse. Then, everything grinds to a halt along with it.

Centuries ago, when we first began to trade with each other, we began to interconnect, and globalization was born. If we knew then about the desire to receive and the desire to give, the history of humanity would be very different from the bloody march of folly it has turned out to be.

Today, it is impossible to "de-globalize" the world. As we showed in Chapter 10, and as the opening quote suggests, we must begin to act as one united humanity, in line with nature's principle of collaboration and self-fulfillment, or life as we know it will end. And the way to unite is to become aware of the two desires and employ both in our negotiations, especially around finances, given today's monetary crisis.

It is not tougher regulation or buying of "toxic assets" that will help us through the present crisis. The way out is to understand that what needs to be regulated is human nature, not the economy. Our economy is only a projection of our one-track minds: receiving, receiving, and more receiving.

Today, humanity must come to realize that it is in our best interest to consider others in our plans, or else those plans will fail. Therefore, the first step in the financial bailout plan should be to share information and provide facts about the kind of world we live in, which is global and inter-dependent.

People should know that there are two forces running the world. The first is the desire to re-ceive, which economists call "the profit-oriented economy," meaning capitalism. The second force is the desire to give, which aims to increase general prosperity and well-being.

Simply put, in today's financial dealings, *everyone must profit* or no one will profit. To be exact, the term, "everyone," does not refer to the parties involved in a contract, but to the *entire world*.

Does that mean that before every new deal or agreement, the parties must knock on the door of every home in the world, explain the proposed deal, and ask for a signed consent to it? This would hardly be practical. All it means is that we must change our attitude towards considering *everyone's* benefit instead of *ours* alone.

For example, whenever a new product is launched, the manufacturer immediately seeks to outdo its competitors. The new company aims to increase its market share, and we call this process, "capitalism." However, at the end of the day, what is really happening is an attempt to "steal" customers from those already in the market. This is the accepted norm.

Similarly, banks today are not committed to boosting the faltering economy or assisting people who want to start businesses or buy homes. Banks want only one thing: to make as much money as they can for their shareholders (owners/directors). And if they have to pay their lower-ranking employees shameful wages, or grant people criminally irresponsible loans and then sell those loans to insurance companies, which then try to toss the hot potato until someone finally gets stuck with it, it's all part of "business as usual." Their only aim is to write billions on the plus column at the end of every quarter.

And this attitude is not the sole property of banks. Essentially, every business operates this way, from insurance companies, through banks and hedge funds, down to the mom-and-pop grocery stores. We call it the "free market."

Today, however, we must *all* undertake a serious inspection of our system to see where we have gone wrong. When we do so, we will see that there is nothing wrong with the idea of having banks or insurance companies in our world. Banks are potentially a good thing, because without them we could not finance our dreams. Insurance companies are also positive forces because they guarantee that we will not be thrown out on the street, should something go wrong in our lives.

Therefore, all that needs to change is the business' goal—from benefitting itself, at the expense of its competitors, to benefitting the whole of society. We should plan our financial dealings in such a way that the net profits will go toward promoting humanity, instead of the business. In business, as in politics, protectionism is a double-edged sword, which punishes its operator far worse than its intended target.

When TV, arts, and schools change the social atmosphere to one of caring and camaraderie, accolade will be a prize worth winning. Then, instead of the current profit-oriented system, the reward for benefitting society will be social recognition and appreciation.

Thus, if all of us aim to benefit more than just ourselves or our shareholders, we and all our customers will prosper because people will trust each other. Clearly, where money is concerned, trust is paramount.Currently, banks have no trust in other banks. Insurance companies also have no trust in banks, or in each other, and no one trusts the borrowers, because borrowers cannot trust their employers to not fire them the next day, because the employers themselves are dependent on market demand, and no one trusts the market these days.

This brings us back to the first point: studying nature's laws. We are not going to trust each other until we understand how we, and the whole of reality, are formulated. Then, we can *collectively* decide to follow that inner formula of balance. When we do, borrowers will trust their employers, who will trust the banks, who will trust the insurance companies, and everyone will trust the market.

Thus, until we learn to function as one big *united* human family, we will not recover from the recession. But when we do, we will not only have everything we need for comfortable living, we will be secure in knowing that we will have it in the future, and so will our children and our children's children.

13

TEACH YOUR CHILDREN WELL

"This crippling of individuals I consider the worst evil of capitalism. Our whole educational system suffers from this evil. An exaggerated competitive attitude is inculcated into the student, who is trained to worship acquisitive success as a preparation."

--Albert Einstein

In Webster's dictionary, education means "the action or process of educating or of being educated [schooled/informed]." But in a world where fifty percent of what we learn in the first year of college is outdated and irrelevant by the end of the third year, what good is our schooling?

Even more important, with the escalating global crisis, can we guarantee our children's education, even through high school? Because the current crisis is global and multi-faceted, the education system must adapt itself and prepare our youth to cope with the current state of the world.

Therefore, our challenge today is not so much to acquire knowledge as it is to acquire the social skills to help ourselves and our children overcome the abundant alienation, suspicion, and mistrust we encounter today. To prepare our children for life in the 21st century, we must first teach them what makes our reality what it is, and what they can do to change it.

This does not mean that disseminating knowledge should stop, but that these lessons should be part of a larger story that teaches students how to cope in the world they are about to enter. They should be able to leave the classroom and use this knowledge to grasp the full picture of reality and the forces that design it, and to understand how they can use it to their benefit.

In nearly every country in the world, education systems are designed to prod students to aim for personal achievements. The higher the student's grades, the higher his or her social status. In America, as in many countries in the West, this system not only measures how students perform, but how they perform *in relation to others*. This makes students not only want to excel, but inevitably makes them want their fellow students to fail.

In a globalized world where every person is dependent on the success and well-being of every other person, this system must be reformed from its roots. Instead of trying to achieve personal distinction, the objective should be to excel in promoting the success of the collective. This is the achievement that should ideally be most recognized and revered.

And the means to encouraging students to contribute to society is the environment. Just as the media should stop extolling the ultra rich, schools should stop extolling the ultra individualists, who strive only for their own success. And just as the media should praise those who promote others, schools should praise students who excel in promoting other students.

Therefore, the first thing to change in every school must be its atmosphere. There need not be a punishment system for the more self-centered students, since society has such an overwhelming influence over youth that they will follow the social code almost instinctively. Instead, an atmosphere of camaraderie and sharing should prevail. This can be promoted by encouraging peer tutoring, where students work to help and promote each other, and receive social recognition in return.

Additionally, there are many exercises that require teamwork to succeed. Those can be applied very easily to the existing curricula, with grades given to groups rather than to individuals. In this way, one student's grades will depend on the performance of all the others in the group.

In fact, looking at the adult world, we see that seldom is a product manufactured by a single person. And even in such cases, great teamwork is required for them to succeed. Indeed, nature and our own lives teach us how important it is to collaborate, so why not begin at school?

If children today grow violent and disobedient despite our efforts to raise them to be humane and caring, we can change this pattern by creating schools where children depend on each other to succeed. This can create a new sense of caring for each other and eliminate previously self-centered patterns.

For children, interdependency is as natural as breathing. Starting from birth, a child depends on its parents for everything it needs to survive. By the time children enter school, their social needs develop and they become completely reliant on others' approval to maintain a positive self-image.

As a result, they feel the power of society over them so strongly that, given an atmosphere of caring, it will require very little effort for us to rear caring youths. All we will need to do is show them the right direction, one that will lead to success for them and for humanity, and they will lead the way.

The first thing we must do is teach them how nature works—that there are two forces that interact in their lives, and that for everyone to be happy, these forces must be in balance. We need change nothing about the topics we teach; we only need to add that B element to the curriculum: Balance.

Thus, biology will still be biology, flavored with an explanation of how the interplay between the forces of giving and receiving led to the development of multi-cellular creatures from single-celled creatures. The same applies to physics and to all the hard sciences. With humanities, it will be truly refreshing to examine human history and various societies with the interplay of desires in the forefront.

Though it is beyond the scope of this book to do so, one can easily see how we progress as our desires change and intensify. Without such changing and growing desires, we would have no revolutions because we would not want to change our lives. We would also have no technology because we would settle for what we have. We would have no politics (actually, this may not be a bad idea), and no rules. In all likelihood, if we didn't change our desires, we would still be living in caves.

There are two stages to building a school that promotes the element of balance:

1. **Providing information:** Schools should teach the students about the desire to give and the desire to receive, and how these forces work together in nature. This should be done in both specifically designated classes and as a part of every topic in the school curriculum.

2. **Establishing new social norms:** After children have acquired a basic understanding of the concepts, we should gradually establish social norms that promote collaboration, friendship, and support.

   For this stage to succeed, it is very important that children understand that they are not following these precepts because adults are forcing them upon them. Instead, they must constantly be made aware that they will fare best in life with an approach that is in sync with nature. Hence, it is in their best personal interests to follow this approach.

To survive in today's world, we must know how to interact with each other as collaborators, not as combatants. Otherwise, everything we do will fail. By teaching the art of collaboration and sharing, we will do our children the best service possible because we will be equipping them with the most important tool they need for life's challenges.

No one else will equip them with this tool if we shirk our responsibility to give it to them. By using the social environment to create schools that aim to teach students how to live in the global age, to share, to care, and to take both life forces into consideration in their every action, we are creating the only kind of school worth attending.

14

Yes, We Can (and Must)

"Mankind will never see an end of trouble until... lovers of wisdom come to hold political power, or the holders of power... become lovers of wisdom."

--Plato, *The Republic*

The change proposed in this book is not a superficial one, but a fundamental change that goes beyond how we build our economic system, our education system, or even our political system. It is a change in our understanding of life, and as a result, of the society we live in. For the change to last, we need to realize that at our stage in human development, we as individuals cannot prosper unless the whole world prospers, too.

In the past, it was enough to be good to our families. By doing so, we balanced ourselves with the giving force of nature on the only level we were conscious of—our families.

Afterwards, as our communities grew, we needed to become aware of larger groups, and we learned that it is not enough to be good to one's family, but also to offer care and kindness to one's townspeople. This put us in balance with the giving force at the community level.

Then, we grew even more and needed to balance ourselves with nature's giving force on the national level, beyond that of our towns or families.

Today, we need to do the same towards the whole world. Our awareness, whether or not we are conscious of it, now encompasses all of humanity. Hence, to balance ourselves with the giving force in nature, we must be positive and contribute to everyone, everywhere.

The consequence of not doing so is the crisis we see unfolding before our eyes. It is not a punishment from some higher force, but a natural result of not obeying a natural law, similar to the pain we feel when we disobey the law of gravity and jump off a roof without proper preparation or equipment. For us humans, our best defense is awareness.

And because awareness of nature's desire to give is our first and most important tool, the first thing we must do is to teach politicians about its role and importance. We must show them that we haven't been aware of it thus far, and that its absence from our thoughts is the cause of today's crisis. In this way, politicians, who are highly sensitive to what works and what doesn't, will know how and why they need to change their policies to suit today's requirements.

Since politicians and statespersons live every day in the self-centered system of politics, they will quickly become aware of the discrepancies between the flawed existing system and the perfect, balanced one. In fact, this process began spontaneously the minute the financial crisis erupted.

Barack Obama's speech on January 20, 2009 at the Ebenezer Baptist Church in Atlanta, Georgia, is a beautiful example of such awareness: "Unity is the great need of the hour—the great need of this hour. Not because it sounds pleasant or because it makes us feel good, but because it's the only way we can overcome the essential deficit that exists in this country. I'm not talking about a budget deficit. I'm not talking about a trade deficit. I'm not talking about a deficit of good ideas or new plans. I'm talking about a moral deficit. I'm talking about an empathy deficit. I'm taking about an inability to recognize ourselves in one another; to understand that we are our brother's keeper; we are our sister's keeper; that... we are all tied together in a single garment of destiny."

In light of that reckoning, all we need to do is add the adhesive, the substance that will make that garment strong, yet soft and smooth. And that substance is the awareness that in uniting, we are aligning with the giving force in nature.

Achieving unity among politicians does not mean an end to debates and conflicts, but with both desires of nature in mind, conflicts can become fertile ground for change. As public opinion changes via the media, as described in Chapter 10, politicians will not worry about losing votes because they've lost political arguments. On the contrary, if a politician is able to change his or her view after realizing that it is in the public's interest to take another direction, constituents will consider this flexibility an act of strength.

Moreover, in doing so, that politician becomes even more responsible for the success of the new direction, having seriously debated its pros and cons before deciding in its favor. The politician can then tell voters, "Look, I have weighed the options and have concluded that my opponent's idea will be of greater benefit to the public than mine. Therefore, I think you should support it."

This is a big responsibility, bigger even than that of the "winner" of the debate. By taking this approach, not only is unity enhanced, but ideas are thought through much more thoroughly.

International politics will have to change in the same way, too. In the global age, caring for the world is far more important than caring only for one's country. Naturally, this trend must be shared by all the nations if it is to succeed. It requires that everyone knows about the two desires that sustain the foundations of our world. Without this knowledge, isolation and protectionism will prevail and wars will erupt. With it, we will finally have a genuine opportunity to achieve world peace.

15

BEING WELL
AND STAYING WELL

"Half of the modern drugs could well be thrown out of the window, except that the birds might eat them."

--Dr. Martin Henry Fischer

Thousands of years ago, in ancient China, medicine was practiced quite opposite to the way it is practiced today. In those days, every household put a vase outside its door. As the healer made his daily rounds through the houses of the village, he would look into each vase. If there was a coin inside it, he took the coin and went on his way, knowing that everyone in the house was healthy.

If the vase was empty, the healer knew that someone inside was ill. He would enter and treat the patient to the best of his ability. When the sick person was well again, the daily payment of a coin resumed.

This was a simple method that guaranteed the healer's interest in the health of his patients, for his payments continued as long as the patient was well. To maximize his profits, the healer needed the people under his supervision to stay healthy as much of the time as possible. For this reason, the healer would walk around the village in his free time, advise people on healthy living, and reprimand those who were negligent. If a person was stubborn and refused to lead a wholesome way of life, the healer would exclude him from his rounds and refuse him medical attention when he needed it.

This simple method guaranteed that both patient and healer had a vested interest in keeping healthy—a stark difference from our present approach to medicine.

In modern medicine, a physician's salary is comprised of how many patients are treated daily, how many commissions are given by drug manufacturers, and how high the doctor's rates are for services. Under private medicine, wealthier patients pay more for better doctors, which produces a skew in the quality of care available to those in lower income brackets.

In addition, today's system penalizes a physician whose patients are healthy. In fact, the practitioner could theoretically starve to death or get a pink slip precisely because he or she has succeeded in keeping people healthy!

The drug companies, which we hail whenever they announce a new drug or treatment for an illness, are trapped in that same circle. If they produced a drug that actually made people well, they would go bankrupt. Hence, it is in their interest that we remain alive and unwell. The whole system—hospitals, drug companies, doctors, nurses, and caretakers—actually benefits from perpetuating our ill health. It is the only way healthcare workers can sustain themselves.

But this reality is not the fault of any one person. Doctors are not evil people, at least no more than you and I. They are trapped in a system that has been built to maximize profit instead of health and well-being. As a result, patients—ordinary people—must protect themselves by purchasing costly health insurance and depend on the judicial system in cases of malpractice.

This, in turn, forces physicians to buy costly insurance policies to protect themselves against malpractice suits. This whole system reflects a very sick situation!

And what evildoer has created this broken system? It is our own ignorance of nature. Indeed, the healthcare system is perhaps where the symptoms of seeing only one half of reality manifest most acutely.

HEALING THE HEALTHCARE SYSTEM

Clearly, we cannot emulate the ancient Chinese healthcare system. We have grown too entangled in our egotistical systems to untangle them without causing the whole system to collapse. The Chinese model, however, can serve as an example of how simple, inexpensive, and health-promoting our healthcare system should be.

No one understands balance better than physicians. In medicine, this state is called "homeostasis." Webster's Dictionary defines it as "a relatively stable state of equilibrium or a tendency toward such a state between the different but interdependent elements or groups of elements of an organism."

Remember the rule of collaboration and self-fulfillment we talked about in Chapter 10? In medicine, it is expressed as the last part of this definition: "different but interdependent elements or groups of elements of an organism."

Homeostasis is also what defines health or illness within the body. Thus, physicians can easily grasp the concept. Hence, studying both of nature's qualities—giving and receiving—is the first thing to do. This will create an awareness and a sense of urgency to change today's lame system.

Anyone who ever studied biology knows that a healthy cell gives its utmost support to its host organism, and in return receives its sustenance and protection from the organism. A cancerous cell does just the opposite—it takes all it can from the organism and gives it nothing in return. As a result, the host is consumed and dies along with the cancer.

For this reason, researchers and physicians are the best candidates for a conscious change of heart. They will understand the need for mutual guarantee among all members of humanity better than anyone. And they will also understand that the days of today's system are numbered, and that the need for change is imminent and pressing.

Just like the immune system in a body, health-care workers' job is to keep people healthy, as well as to treat them once they are sick. And the workers' reward for people's health should be the praise of society. Of course, they should receive proper wages to allow them a life of dignity, but beyond that, their reward should come from society's recognition.

As with every other type of change, its success depends on the social atmosphere. In an atmosphere of self-centeredness, this shift will never succeed. But in an atmosphere of camaraderie and trust, it is certain to succeed.

Because of the complexity of today's healthcare system, it is vital that all its participants will not only be aware of the need for change, but will want to realize it simultaneously. Then, just as the symptoms of humanity's illness appear most acutely in the healthcare system, healing will manifest itself most dramatically in precisely that system.

16

... AND STAYING COOL

"Till now man has been up against Nature; from now on he will be up against his own nature."

--Dennis Gabor, *Inventing the Future*, 1964

On the surface, ecology should be the easiest topic to address in this book. Make all cars electric, all power plants solar or wind powered, and make all plastic recyclable. Then, voila, the world is a green, beautiful, and cool place once again. But if it's that easy, why haven't we succeeded so far?

There are many answers to that question. The most obvious is that we have been so busy making money from fossil fuels and cheap plastics, we have put everything else aside, including the planet—our home and that of our children. Another plausible answer is that solar energy is simply inefficient and costly, and using it would raise the price of electricity so high, it would be too expensive for people to use.

Yet, all these problems focus on the technicalities and leave aside the real issue—our indifference to the future of our earthly home and our intolerance of the needs of others. In short, as Dr. Gabor so plainly said, the real problem is human nature.

Today, our inaction about the state of our planet is almost criminal: we are subjecting parts of the world to floods that ruin the crops they live on, and we are afflicting other parts of the world with such severe droughts that people are simply dying of thirst. So why are we so heartless toward nature and towards ourselves?

The answer is that we have forgotten our primordial root—the balance of forces between the desire to give and the desire to receive. We see this balance in all of nature's levels: the inanimate, vegetative, and animal. We humans consider ourselves above nature, perhaps not in theory but certainly in practice. But the truth is that we are not above it at all. We are very much a part of it.

We are the speaking level, the most highly developed level of nature. As such, we are also the most influential part of it: our actions affect all other levels of nature. But more important, our internal condition affects the rest of nature just as powerfully as our actions affect it, if not more. And when our internal condition is one of imbalance, egotism, and unawareness of the giving force in nature, the whole of nature falls into egotism and unawareness of the giving force, and everyone suffers—plants, animals, and people.

For this reason, even if we all drive electric vehicles and use only energy from renewable sources, the world will not become more welcoming. What will make the difference is if we recognize the desire to give, and learn how to incorporate it into our lives.

Consider this: when we suffer from such a mild annoyance as a common cold, it affects our whole body. We cannot breathe easily, we lose our appetites, our temperatures rise, we become weak, and our concentration drops. Similarly, the world is like a small village, and everything we do affects everyone and everything else. Hence, we must learn about nature's balance at the most fundamental level—the level of desires—and implement it in our lives.

This does not mean that if I help an old lady cross the street, a hurricane will stop blowing in the Atlantic. It means that if we *all* think of everyone else's good at least as much as we think of our own, because we want to get to know the giving force, then all of us together will make suffering a thing of the past.

It may sound fantastic, but if you remember that the only inharmonious and disruptive element in nature is us, it makes perfect sense that when we are united in harmony and in equilibrium, the hell that our planet is becoming will reverse itself.

And the most beautiful part about it is that we will not have to do a thing to make this happen. It will happen by itself, because our newly balanced senses will guide us correctly as to how to manage ourselves and create a heaven on earth.

This is as true for ecology as it is for economy, education, health, and every other aspect of our lives.

17

Epilogue

I titled this book, *Bail Yourself Out: How You Can Emerge Strong from the World Crisis*, because today we cannot rely on others to do it for us. And the irony about the title, as you might have sensed, is that although the only way out of the crisis is to work together, the decision to act this way lies with each and every person.

As we have been saying throughout the book, the universe is built on the balance between two forces—the desire to give and the desire to receive. And because these forces lay beneath all that exists, every element in the universe must maintain that balance within it. Objects and creatures that do not maintain it within them cannot survive.

In the animal kingdom, animals eat only what they need and leave the rest untouched. In this way, they naturally maintain nature's balance by grazing where there is plenty of grass and leaving depleted areas, or by preying only on weak or sick animals. This is how nature preserves and promotes the wellness of the stronger and healthier plants and animals.

But man is a different story. Through our connections with each other, we desire to receive not only from nature, like animals, but also from other people. And when we begin to exploit others, we are no longer aligned with nature's two forces because we are over-using the desire to receive and under-using the desire to give.

In this way, we undermine the balance of the two forces that form life, and thus disrupt the whole of nature. The multiple crises we are faced with today are in fact manifestations of this very disorder: the imbalance we inflict on nature. If we learn to balance these desires within us—take what we need and give the rest to nature and to humanity—we will immediately restore the balance, and all systems will stabilize, like a sick person who has suddenly been cured.

As we said in Chapter 10, at all levels of creation, from the atomic to the most complex human relations, existence is possible only through collaboration and self-fulfillment. Thus, for the survival of humanity, all of us must realize our personal potential through our contribution to the societies we live in. And today, that society is the entire world.

Toward the second decade of the 21st century, it is becoming increasingly clear that the days of personal, self-centered success are drawing to a close. Since the 19th century, the predominant school of economics has been the "economic human" (Homo Economicus), which builds its guidelines on the concept that we humans are "self-interested actors."

In order to reverse this negative trend and to quickly heal the world, we need to make a small but paramount amendment: "economic *humanity*." The new guidelines should rely on humans being *collective*-interested actors.

The minute we change our attitude toward benefitting one another, we will correct what has been wrong since the time of Babel, and the effect will be immediate. Today, every scientist, politician, economist, and businessperson knows that we are all interdependent. This is why every world leader, from Obama to Brown to Putin, is preaching unity these days. But it takes *everyone* to succeed—each and every person in the world. We are all under nature's law of balance; hence, it is truly everyone's responsibility.

In conclusion, I'd like to hitch this wagon to a star and suggest that to bail ourselves out, each of us need not ask what the world can do for me, but what I can do for the world.

ABOUT THE AUTHOR

Michael Laitman, PhD, is a professor of Ontology, a PhD in Philosophy and Kabbalah, and an MSc in medical Bio-cybernetics. He is founder and president of Bnei Baruch and Ashlag Research Institute (ARI), two Israel based international educational organizations with branches all over North America and Canada, Central and South America, as well as Eastern and Western Europe.

On his website, **www.kab.info**, he teaches free, live daily lessons on Kabbalah and spirituality to an audience of approximately two million people worldwide, simultaneously broadcast and translated into eight languages: English, Spanish, Hebrew, Italian, Russian, French, Turkish, and German. Prof. Laitman also presents regularly on Channel 66, which is distributed by Israel's Satellite TV provider, YES.

ABOUT BNEI BARUCH

Bnei Baruch is a group of Kabbalists in Israel, sharing the wisdom of Kabbalah with the entire world. Study materials in over 30 languages are based on authentic Kabbalah texts that were passed down from generation to generation.

History and Origin

In 1991, following the passing of his teacher, The Rabash, Michael Laitman established a Kabbalah study group called "Bnei Baruch." Laitman had been The Rabash's prime student and personal assistant, and is recognized as the successor of Rabash's teaching method.

The Rabash was the firstborn son and successor of Baal HaSulam (1884-1954), the greatest Kabbalist of the 20th century. Baal HaSulam authored the most authoritative and comprehensive commentary on *The Book of Zohar*, titled *The Sulam* (Ladder) *Commentary*. He was the first to reveal the complete method for spiritual ascent.

Today, Bnei Baruch bases its entire study method on the path paved by these two great spiritual leaders.

The Study Method

The unique study method developed by Baal HaSulam, and his son, the Rabash, is taught and applied on a daily basis by Bnei Baruch. This method relies on authentic Kabbalah sources such as *The Book of Zohar*, by Rabbi Shimon Bar-Yochai, *The Tree of Life*, by the Ari, and *The Study of the Ten Sefirot*, by Baal HaSulam.

While the study relies on authentic Kabbalah sources, it is carried out in simple language and uses a scientific, contemporary approach. Developing this approach has made Bnei Baruch an internationally respected organization, both in Israel and in the world at large.

The unique joining of an academic study method and personal experiences broadens the students' perspective and awards them a new perception of the reality they live in. Those on the spiritual path are given the necessary tools to study themselves and their surrounding reality.

The Message

Bnei Baruch is a diverse movement of hundreds of thousands of students worldwide. The essence of the message disseminated by Bnei Baruch is universal: unity of the people, unity of nations and love of man.

For millennia, Kabbalists have been teaching that love of man should be the foundation of all human relations. This love prevailed in the days of Abraham and the group of Kabbalists that he established. If we make room for these seasoned, yet contemporary values, we will discover that we possess the power to put differences aside and unite.

The wisdom of Kabbalah, hidden for millennia, has been waiting for the time when we would be sufficiently developed and ready to implement its message. Now, it is emerging as a solution that can unite diverse factions everywhere, enabling us, as individuals and as a society, to meet today's challenges.

Activities

Bnei Baruch was established on the premise that "only by expansion of the wisdom of Kabbalah to the public can the world be saved from extinction" (Baal HaSulam). Hence, Bnei Baruch offers a variety of ways for people to explore nature and their lives, providing careful guidance for beginners and advanced students alike.

Television

Bnei Baruch established a production company, ARI Films, **www.arifilms.tv**, specializing in production of educational TV programs throughout the world, and in many languages.

In Israel, Bnei Baruch established its own channel, aired through cable and satellite 24/7.

All broadcasts on the channel are free of charge. Programs are adapted for all levels, from complete beginners to the most advanced.

Internet

Bnei Baruch's website, **www.kab.info**, presents the authentic wisdom of Kabbalah using essays, books, and original texts. It is by far the most expansive source of authentic Kabbalah material on the net, containing a unique, extensive library for readers to thoroughly explore the wisdom of Kabbalah.

Bnei Baruch's online Learning Center offers unique, free Kabbalah lessons for beginners, initiating students into this profound body of knowledge in the comfort of their own homes.

Bnei Baruch's TV channel is aired on the Internet at **www.kab.tv**, offering, among other programs, Prof. Laitman's daily lessons, complete with texts and diagrams.

All these services are provided free of charge.

Books

Bnei Baruch publishes authentic Kabbalah books. These books are essential for complete understanding of authentic Kabbalah, explained in Prof. Laitman's lessons.

Laitman writes his books in a clear, contemporary style based on the concepts of Baal HaSulam. These books are a vital link between today's readers and the original texts. All the books are available for sale at **www.kabbalahbooks.info**, as well as for free download.

Funding

Bnei Baruch is a not-for-profit organization for teaching and sharing the wisdom of Kabbalah. To maintain its independence and purity of intentions, Bnei Baruch is not supported, funded, or otherwise tied to any government or political organization.

Since the bulk of its activity is provided free of charge, the prime sources of funding for the group's activities are donations and tithing—contributed by students on a voluntary basis—and Laitman's books, which are sold at cost.

How to Contact Bnei Baruch

Bnei Baruch USA,
2009 85th street, #51,
Brooklyn, NY 11214,
USA

1057 Steeles Avenue West, Suite 532
Toronto, ON, M2R 3X1
Canada

E-mail: info@kabbalah.info
Web site: www.kab.info

Toll free in USA and Canada:
1-866-LAITMAN
Fax: 1-905 886 9697

OTHER BOOKS BY
LAITMAN KABBALAH PUBLISHERS

From Chaos to Harmony

Many researchers and scientists agree that the ego is the reason behind the perilous state our world is in today. Laitman's groundbreaking book not only demonstrates that egoism has been the basis for all suffering throughout human history, but also shows how we can turn our plight to pleasure.

The book contains a clear analysis of the human soul and its problems, and provides a "roadmap" of what we need to do to once again be happy. *From Chaos to Harmony* explains how we can rise to a new level of existence on personal, social, national, and international levels.

Kabbalah Revealed

This is the most clearly written, reader-friendly guide to making sense of the surrounding world. Each of its six chapters focuses on a different aspect of the wisdom of Kabbalah, illuminating its teachings and explaining them using various examples from our day-to-day lives.

The first three chapters in *Kabbalah Revealed* explain why the world is in a state of crisis, how our growing desires promote progress as well as alienation, and why the biggest deterrent to achieving positive change is rooted in our own spirits. Chapters Four through Six offer a prescription for positive change. In these chapters, we learn how we can use our spirits to build a personally peaceful life in harmony with all of Creation.

Together Forever

On the surface, *Together Forever* is a children's story. But like all good children's stories, it transcends boundaries of age, culture, and upbringing.

In *Together Forever*, the author tells us that if we are patient and endure the trials we encounter along our life's path, we will become stronger, braver, and wiser. Instead of growing weaker, we will learn to create our own magic and our own wonders as only a magician can.

In this warm, tender tale, Michael Laitman shares with children and parents alike some of the gems and charms of the spiritual world. The wisdom of Kabbalah is filled with spellbinding stories. *Together Forever* is yet another gift from this ageless source of wisdom, whose lessons make our lives richer, easier, and far more fulfilling.

Attaining the Worlds Beyond

From the introduction to *Attaining the Worlds Beyond*: "...Not feeling well on the Jewish New Year's Eve of September 1991, my teacher called me to his bedside and handed me his notebook, saying, 'Take it and learn from it.' The following morning, he perished in my arms, leaving me and many of his other disciples without guidance in this world.

"He used to say, 'I want to teach you to turn to the Creator, rather than to me, because He is the only strength, the only Source of all that exists, the only one who can really help you, and He awaits your prayers for help. When you seek help in your search for freedom from the bondage of this world, help in elevating yourself above this world, help in finding the self, and help in determining your purpose in life, you must turn to the Creator, who sends you all those aspirations in order to compel you to turn to Him.'"

Attaining the Worlds Beyond holds within it the content of that notebook, as well as other inspiring texts. This book reaches out to all those seekers who want to find a logical, reliable way to understand the world's phenomena. This fascinating introduction to the wisdom of Kabbalah will enlighten the mind, invigorate the heart, and move readers to the depths of their souls.

Kabbalah for Beginners

Kabbalah for Beginners is a book for all those seeking answers to life's essential questions. We all want to know why we are here, why there is pain, and how we can make life more enjoyable. The four parts of this book provide us with reliable answers to these questions, as well as clear explanations of the gist of Kabbalah and its practical implementations.

Part One discusses the discovery of the wisdom of Kabbalah, and how it was developed, and finally concealed until our time. Part Two introduces the gist of the wisdom of Kabbalah, using ten easy drawings to help us understand the structure of the spiritual worlds, and how they relate to our world. Part Three reveals Kabbalistic concepts that are largely unknown to the public, and Part Four elaborates on practical means you and I can take, to make our lives better and more enjoyable for us and for our children.

Kabbalah, Science, and the Meaning of Life

Science explains the mechanisms that sustain life; Kabbalah explains why life exists. In *Kabbalah, Science, and the Meaning of Life*, Rav Laitman combines science and spirituality in a captivating dialogue that reveals life's meaning.

For thousands of years Kabbalists have been writing that the world is a single entity divided into separate beings. Today the cutting-edge science of quantum physics states a very similar idea: that at the most fundamental level of matter, we are all literally one.

Science proves that reality is affected by the observer who examines it; and so does Kabbalah. But Kabbalah makes an even bolder statement: even the Creator, the Maker of reality, is within the observer. In other words, God is inside of us; He doesn't exist anywhere else. When we pass away, so does He.

These earthshaking concepts and more are eloquently introduced so that even readers new to Kabbalah or science will easily understand them. Therefore, if you're just a little curious about why you are here, what life means, and what you can do to enjoy it more, this book is for you.

Awakening to Kabbalah

A distinctive, personal, and awe-filled introduction to an ancient wisdom tradition. In this book,

Rav Laitman offers a deeper understanding of the fundamental teachings of Kabbalah, and how you can use its wisdom to clarify your relationship with others and the world around you.

Using language both scientific and poetic, he probes the most profound questions of spirituality and existence. This provocative, unique guide will inspire and invigorate you to see beyond the world as it is and the limitations of your everyday life, become closer to the Creator, and reach new depths of the soul.

Basic Concepts in Kabbalah

This is a book to help readers cultivate an approach to the concepts of Kabbalah, to spiritual objects, and to spiritual terms. By reading and re-reading in this book, one develops internal observations, senses, and approaches that did not previously exist within. These newly acquired observations are like sensors that "feel" the space around us that is hidden from our ordinary senses.

Hence, Basic Concepts in Kabbalah is intended to foster the contemplation of spiritual terms. Once we are integrated with these terms, we can begin to see, with our inner vision, the unveiling of the spiritual structure that surrounds us, almost as if a mist has been lifted.

This book is not aimed at the study of facts. Instead, it is a book for those who wish to awaken the deepest and subtlest sensations they can possess.

The Science of Kabbalah

Kabbalist and scientist Rav Michael Laitman, PhD, designed this book to introduce readers to the special language and terminology of the authentic wisdom of Kabbalah. Here, Rav Laitman reveals authentic Kabbalah in a manner both rational and mature. Readers are gradually led to understand the logical design of the Universe and the life that exists in it.

The Science of Kabbalah, a revolutionary work unmatched in its clarity, depth, and appeal to the intellect, will enable readers to approach the more technical works of Baal HaSulam (Rabbi Yehuda Ashlag), such as *The Study of the Ten Sefirot* and *The Book of Zohar*. Readers of this book will enjoy the satisfying answers to the riddles of life that only authentic Kabbalah provides. Travel through the pages and prepare for an astonishing journey into the Upper Worlds.

Introduction to the Book of Zohar

This volume, along with *The Science of Kabbalah*, is a required preparation for those who wish to understand the hidden message of *The Book of Zohar*. Among the many helpful topics dealt with in this text is an introduction to the "language of roots and branches," without which the stories in *The Zohar* are mere fable and legend. *Introduction to the Book of Zohar* will provide readers with the necessary tools to understand authentic Kabbalah as it was originally meant to be—as a means to attain the Upper Worlds.

The Book of Zohar: annotations to the Ashlag commentary

The Book of Zohar (*The Book of Radiance*) is an age-old source of wisdom and the basis for all Kabbalistic literature. Since its appearance nearly 2,000 years ago, it has been the primary, and often only, source used by Kabbalists.

For centuries, Kabbalah was hidden from the public, which was deemed not yet ready to receive it. However, our generation has been designated by Kabbalists as the first generation that *is* ready to grasp the concepts in *The Zohar*. Now we can put these principles into practice in our lives.

Written in a unique and metaphorical language, *The Book of Zohar* enriches our understanding of reality and widens our worldview. Although the text deals with one subject only—how to relate to the Creator—it approaches it from different angles. This allows each of us to find the particular phrase or word that will carry us into the depths of this profound and timeless wisdom.